In Farrell Greenwald Brenner's playful, cutting *Diatribe from the Library,* books are toxins, grenades, they have bones. Books are typed on cigarette papers and smoked outside of the library. Farrell writes of the burning of books, reminds us that "witch-burning is still in vogue," and hints at the smoldering fires of the Holocaust. All of this feels even more palpable as we enter an era with a president-elect who states that the burning of the U.S. flag should be punishable by the loss of citizenship. What is citizenship? What happens "when your family crosses an ocean"? What is displacement and diaspora—for Jews, Palestinians, African-Americans? Can the library, can the book, heal wounds—"this/is mine/the word/the page/the book"? Farrell's book itself is a kind of antidote: "I wish for you the megaphone into which you can spit that fire/and become a dragon of your own."

**— Becca Shaw Glaser, co-author of** *Mindful Occupation: Rising Up Without Burning Out*


Bursting with playful repetition, Farrell Greenwald Brenner's *Diatribe from the Library* is a storm of lyrical verse. Her collection serves as treatise on the millennial college experience—both in and outside the library—with unconventional odes to the "red solo cup," a sly "Psalm" to "...dark roast, merciful be / Thine earthen beans divine," and a hat's off to the "fairy godmothers," of "JSTOR / and SAGE." Often abandoning traditional form and punctuation, Brenner surprises us often with this smart and charming debut.

**— Christina Quintana, author of** *The Heart Wants*

# Diatribe *from the* Library

# Diatribe
*from the*
# Library

Farrell Greenwald Brenner

HEADMISTRESS PRESS

Copyright © 2017 by Farrell Greenwald Brenner
All rights reserved.

ISBN-13: 978-0997914986
ISBN-10: 099791498X

This book may not be reproduced, in whole or in part, including illustrations, in any form (beyond that permitted by Sections 107 and 108 of the U.S. Copyright Law and except by reviewers for the public press), without written permission from the publishers.

Cover art © 2016 Jessica Burke. *Myopic Green Knight* 24" x 18" Prismacolor on Fabriano Tiziano 160g (Billiard Green). jessicaburkeartist.com
Back cover photo of Farrell Greenwald Brenner © 2016 Genevieve Pilch.
Cover & book design by Mary Meriam.

PUBLISHER
Headmistress Press
60 Shipview Lane
Sequim, WA 98382
Telephone: 917-428-8312
Email: headmistresspress@gmail.com
Website: headmistresspress.blogspot.com

# Contents

| | |
|---|---|
| red solo cup garden | 1 |
| Diatribe from the Library | 2 |
| Prevention | 4 |
| Dust | 5 |
| Craters | 6 |
| Library Smokers | 7 |
| Paint these hills | 9 |
| Courted by the Snow | 10 |
| Cite this Poem: a performance in plagiarism | 11 |
| Blessing | 12 |
| Doodles | 14 |
| Psalm | 16 |
| Sit Sleep Walk | 17 |
| Burial | 19 |
| On Reading | 20 |
| Mourning After | 22 |
| eden undone | 23 |
| A Rage | 25 |
| Be Safe | 26 |
| The Tale End | 28 |
| Dead Sea Blues | 29 |
| DS 135 .P64 1893 | 30 |
| | |
| *About the Author* | 33 |
| *Notes* | 34 |
| *Acknowledgments* | 35 |

## red solo cup garden

In the red solo cup garden
a lily quietly blooms
her plastic petals bent     p a t i e n t
through the smoky night
speckled with Dew Drops Lite
The shoelace ivy, impish, creeps
to peekaboo
with a galloping laugh which trips over itself
laughter which tumbles
over grapes in a waterfall
laughter that knows it's out too late
(the air is crispest at two, chewiest at three)
The Ghosts of Guinness Past
shards of iridescent glass
they have been sown
and in one week's time shall sprout anew
And though the gnomes may scowl
(there are deadlines, pulled taught, approaching)
they preside with some granite pride
over the red solo cup garden

# Diatribe from the Library

These glasses ain't for you mister
These crossed legs, this bent wrist neither
I dance under the sultry flickering fluorescent lights
to the punctuation of a printer
You might be confused, mister
by the smile sprouting, lurking on my lips
but it ain't for you, mister
I can read just for me
if I want to
even read too much
if I want to
Just hear me out, mister
Sometimes girls they wanna have
a nice bibliography
for their own damn book
Sometimes they write just to know what their own voice sounds like in their head
So loud the din outside, the roar of the kibitzers
No joke, I promise you, mister
I didn't supplicate myself at this desk, mourner and sepulcher,
for your philological pornographical viewing pleasure
with a leer that bores holes like lasers
Don't you know that book-burning is a crime?
though I suppose witch-burning is still in vogue
I'm talking to you, mister
I wanna know what you got, mister,
what words you stole from me
Dammit, I wannem back, mister
Keep a smart eye over your shoulder
cause I'd give all my books, even my tongue to
see you choke on this bitter apple
You don't get to strut away spotless
watch as this sick ink explodes in your pocket
You thought you could own my verbs
like
sit
and
caress

But I take them back
even as you stare
For so hateful, treacherous, and perverse
are a girl and her words
that they must be picked apart with tedious care
using tweezers and scalpels and incisors
tiny, daily, surgical meals
to feed the gnashing egos of high-end leather loafers

The book I deshelved, cradled,
in my arms transformed into a grenade;
    when I woke up this morning, mister,
        I did not intend on going to war today.

# Prevention

Libraries;
of course, you will, no doubt, at some point encounter them
in your college career
after all
you crazy party animals need to let off some steam
you just need to know how to be safe
how to handle yourself
when under the influence
of course, you will, no doubt, at some point,
read
though try not to do too much at once
you'll get sick
books are
toxins
really
even though they make you feel good
And don't just leave them
lying around where anyone might pick them up
be careful who you trust with
your research it is such a
fragile thing
the first publication so
special
and always walk your friends home
after a long night of studying
some books are
more dangerous than others
depends on where they're grown their density how many bodies
you may feel pressured
to learn words and theories and stories
but there are other, healthier ways

Just say no.

# Dust

*I cannot explain my bones,* she wept to me
as she stitched close another cardboard box
in the process chipping the black nail polish that matched her hair
which once yipped with an electric pink, the color of epiphany and
unguarded laughter.
where does pink hair go to die?
*I cannot explain their creaks, the peppered constellation of scores*
a knoll of cardboard, to be cradled by the movers
and birthed by the shakers
*But the dust,* she smirked dryly, clutching the packing tape like
Judith's sword
*The dust speaks for itself*
*inhabiting our lungs until we speak the dust with every parched*
*exhalation*
*every sigh of discontent*
She held a glass of the purest water up to the light, examining the
refractions
*I am the dust, I think.*
and poured it into another cardboard box, full of packing peanuts
and sat down to sew its lips, to seal the solemn oath
as water seeped through the fleshly pores
This, the woman who once planted a thousand bean sprouts in a
basement
and nourished them with the grace of dust
*Dust is patient, it does not boast*
*In time, all great men will know dust*
*as well as I am acquainted with its*
*comings and goings*
I want to interrupt, scream, beg, where will you go?
Which I realize
is code for
where do I go
after I've swiffered my hands
and forgotten how to breathe with dust in my lungs

a phoenix may be reborn of ashes,
the forest fire cleansing dead parts
but only allergies and sorrow may come of dust

**craters**

how many craters has the moon?
the dips and bumps and edges rough
places where the wax burned low
on cool nights spent waiting at an open window
for another crater
a frost swept in, a shivering moan
*how many craters has the moon?*
a number kept to herself, back turned
i would have to tap her on the shoulder
and seduce her exposure
or else take the blushing orb into my hands
and spin her on her axis myself
in order to count
how many craters has the moon?
but still i would never know
how many craters have the moon.

# Library Smokers

The smokers line up outside the library
muttering to themselves,
*We were promised books. We were promised books.*
But there are none to be had.

Instead there are shelves
and tables and chairs and Adderall
and the luminescent faces of 20-year-old toddlers
And a glass case protects yellowing pages
from the ungodly stare of hungry eyes.

But the books are gone.
Stolen.
Or obsolete.
Same thing.
Irrelevant to mankind.
And birdkind, too.

So as the smokers respire
they conspire
*If we can't have them, nobody can.*
Burn the books, burn down the whole damn library.
Until nothing is left but the blackened and crispy remains of *Roget's Thesaurus*,
the echo of its bones to be displayed alongside the other 'sauruses.

But unfortunately, book-burning
(and arson in general)
is illegal
and therefore could rescind the smokers' right
to stand outside the library in the first place.

So instead of books
they burn themselves
their lung particulates blow away in the wind with each exhalation
a loss of a body part on a molecular level
which carries the message of sadness and protest
*Breathe our burnt, bookless air.*

Because the smokers know that it is worse to live in a world
where there are no books
(or worse, where the books are merely ghosts of books:
out of reach, on a shelf too tall for a reader to grasp,
and the librarian is also a ghost,
whisper-pale,   blister-stale).

And it is sometimes nice to imagine
that instead of nicotine
There are books inscribed on the papers of the cigarettes
And they breathe in the mourned words
never to be read again.

## Paint these hills

You could paint these hills with a million brushes
each distinct in its rendition of the color violet
and never even approach the glowing purple flowing
the
movement of heliotropic space, pushing
outwards like a hatching chick
the
cooled volcanic flood of amethyst,
hardened over the curves of dozing giants
the
crying out and hearing your lilac echoes come back to you,
whispering
*this does not belong to you, it's the other way around*

# Courted by the Snow

I was once courted by the snow
she called on me late at night
climbed up my stairs
tapped at my window
rested against my door
left me little doodles that were both charming and magnificent
and notes saying *good morning angel*
*I will be out today, there is a new milk delivery outside*
*xoxo*
soft like baby's breath
I'd stick out my tongue to taste her
and sharp as the razor blade
I'd wear gloves when we held hands
but even as she fell from the sky
spread-eagle
she would not fall for me
hard to tell where she began and ended
drifting transient
infectious to the last,
glowing
covering
sighing
stopping
stunning everyone
and everything
in their tracks

# Cite This Poem: a performance in plagiarism

Once I smiled in secret at the gossip of the starlings
For you they call, the swaying mass, their eager faces turning;
I said: You killed me ... and I forgot, like you, to die.
we were never meant to survive

That, scarce awake, thy soul shall deem
Lillies that fester smell far worse than weeds.
For the soul is a wanderer with many hands and feet.
And miles to go before I sleep

Death has nothing to do with going away.
There sure are a lot of dangerous birds around.

# Blessing

I wish for you
a thousand butterfly wings
so that every time yours are clipped
inevitably inevitably
you have another pair
and I wish for you the sutures
so that you can put them back on yourself
I wish for you
the soft still magnificence of snow
may it cool you
like a meteorological piña colada
may you never grow scared and slow
in the snow's bitter throe
I wish for you
all the stars in the sky
the misanthropes say they are dead
the Hasidim, merely holes in a scrim
but you were the one who taught me
that they are an EKG we haven't yet learned how to read
I wish for you
an ocean! of ideas seen start to end
that salt you taste?
bitter tears of dragons we defeated long ago
far-off fairy tales you need pay no mind for now
I wish for you
stickers that never fade
and knives that never dull
blankets that never scratch
and men that never say you're being too sensitive
I wonder why that's something they're proud of
the inability to feel all the places on the body
where you've been punched
don't they want to know where the wounds are?
I wish for you
a fire
burning through your throat
that no amount of Tums can cure

I wish for you the megaphone into which you can spit that fire
and become a dragon of your own
I wish for you
your own two eyes
open like a lion's roar
on level with those of the hunter
and a peace with that

# Doodles

Doodles (those gentle tic-tac-toe boards
and logarithmic spirals adrift
penned in corners where they have no business),
a doodle, let to run loose in a canyon,
is the result of one neuron charging and releasing,
acceleration of acceleration increasing,
hurling a message across an abyss of nothing,
praying there is someone standing at the other side
—listening—
and suddenly the entire sky is flooded
with the effulgence of fifty fires
flares flashing across the chasm
connecting the star-crossed lovers
in a single sensation
which
through translation
we understand to be
sight
sound
taste
smell
feeling
reeling
healing
spinning back out into the expanse

For every word I have obscured
with a scratch of obsidian ink
I have written one hundred more
Each one a synonym for my name
traced and retraced like a grave marking
as a reminder that
this
is mine
the word
the page
the book
mine

where everywhere else I am made to supplicate myself
before the thrones of legibility
and credibility
here I reign sovereign subject of my own incorrect republic
reject of a cleaner, neater project
unchecked, I inject
and infect the precious rules of hand
"Bookstore! Hear my messy, unruly demand!"
I demand my mind back
For it was stolen
though we do not call this theft
    You tell me, *she left*
But I know better
I have doodled far better tales in notebook margins
than the one peddled to me on your alabaster stoop

# Psalm

*O dark roast, merciful be*
*Thine earthen beans divine*
*accept this offering*
*of a Parisian kiss*

(Do not confuse the plantation for a playground)

*Praise thee, cup overflowing*
*Filtered and pure*
*Awake me to your creation*
*Fill me with your glory*

(In rhythmic hands and erythematic hearts pulse hungry knives seeking brown fruit)

*I believe in the mug,*
*the creamer, and the Holy Bailey's*
*who only strengthen my resolve*
*latte mocha java, frappe venti affogato, amen.*

## Sit Sleep Walk

I have written poems moralizing bits of painted skin
and the sound of pumps fleeing unevenly down the pavement.
I have exhaled into a megaphone questions of being,
if it is possible for one to truly sit, to sleep, to walk
when one is constantly being fucked
by eyes and silence and Polaroids and interviews and occasionally
even other human bodies.
I have railed on this fuckery
said, I too can sit and sleep and walk even as the highway between
my naval and calves is articulated, in a spit take of stout, as a
receptacle for thrusts of resentment
and disgust
it still counts as sitting and sleeping and walking.
The history of all my words spent pondering the validity of my toes
defending my own existence as a natural occurrence
Time to pick up the shards of glass
even as they nick
How heavy this cracked mirror is now that I grip it, wield it
a shield
which reflects the vitriolic lasers that burn through eyelids, walls,
ribcages
BOOM
*I will take you down with me, a strangling embrace*
CRASH
*I will burn this city to its smoldering foundries before I am sucked into its sewers*
BOOM
You are killing me, us, them, you are taking
and taking
and taking
and soon there will be no more Monopoly money left to finance
your fragility
When you have buried every last Lateisha Green
in the rubble of a wrecked temple to the sacred feminine,
who will you step on to make yourself taller?

Egos of a certain volume leave pieces of themselves behind, hot and tarlike
a trail of crumbs
Who do you think sweeps them up after you every morning, prying the mess off the treads of shoes?
I am not here to kiss better the scratches left on your cheek by feral claws you presumed tamed—
I am licking my own wounds and dipping my fingers in bubbling oil.
first to heal the skin I chewed like tobacco
then to ignite
and catapult
and show you just how cool a cucumber can be

# Burial

Here is the shovel
corroded copper cold
The leaden earth will yield
when asked sweetly
dig hearty, dig deep
We are not planting kind words here
this ain't your gramma's time capsule

Here is the shovel
tire not, halt never
Even when the pebbles of your gall
are scudded downstream

Here is the shovel
and a pair of earmuffs, too
Some find the noises secreted by the dead
disquieting
The tattoos will fleetly fade and
a spine cracked in two
is neatly irreparable

Here is the shovel
whose name is Manashe
a moonlit face is a tempting read
Better put back in the ground
what we couldn't keep on the shelf
There are no eulogies
for the overdue.

# On Reading

My soul is chaperoned by four fairy godmothers
Their names are
Taylor
and Francis
and JSTOR
and SAGE.
They promised me a tomb full of ancient secrets
and the recipe for the ultimate love potion
(to be used sparingly on carefully crafted emails)
they promised me sweet and sexy success
and genius far beyond my wildest dreams
But all I got were reams and reams and reams
of paper
enchanted copy machines
bursting at the seams
with paper

My one wish:
that, like my seagull-grandpa, who soared across the quad's
gentle jade slope,
I too could learn to fly;
with a wave of their wands and a puff of pink smoke,
they turned me into an ostrich
There isn't any sand here, though we have an ashy-khaki snow
…so instead, I stick my head in books
where I can pretend it's warm
the high humming frequency of the vibrations in my head
quiver down my body
tear the pages to shreds
Never again will they be read
They will be subject to no more looks
of those crooks
who dare push their way between the covers
of books

Keep reading
keep        reading
keep              reading
never      stop            reading

lest the light dwindle from your eyes
lest those vibrations slow so you can hear the
white and whispered lies
lest we question your commitment or
your capacity to drink words like shots
too fast to taste
and going to waste
choking on words
don't think just read
swallow, but do not savor
memorize, but do not remember
the bodies buried on the other side of the wall
so that you could make sense of random scratches in the bricks
that once spelled out a forgotten folktale of fugitives and freaks
now lost in a sea of forever-reading basketballing Greeks
It's 27 pages on the triangle slave trade
and another 40 on Venus in retrograde
It's 19 on how fast Black bodies bleed
and seventy-fucking-two more on Edward Said
you see
you misplaced your bookmark
somewhere between *discipline* and *dissent*
(or was it *punish?*)
And when bodies are bleeding out onto our desks
right in front of us
we will be neck-deep in paper
assigned by the professor
who doesn't know how else to get tenure

And
like most fairy tales
at midnight, the jig is up
the library closes
the printer shuts down
I get a heavy piece of stock called a diploma
the next batch of readers
and bleeders
cycle in
and make wishes
and begin making nests out of the shredded paper left in my wake

## Mourning After

It feels as if
fifty ghosts
have walked
straight
through me
they pull me by the navel
say, *come*
*we have been to the somewhere*
*come with us*

i ask WebMD, what does it mean to be trampled
in a world without floors
just the echoes of a bass
a pulse
ringing in my aching head

words

                        flee

          me

                                            as

                                                              blood might

Survivor's guilt is a communicable disease
more terrifying than your panic
than your drugless virus
than our softest kisses
however abominable they may be

## eden undone

Adam's ale flowed down the hallway like a burst dam
drowning his darling Steve
who some of you know as Estefan
while Lilith fucked restless, doe-eyed Eve
(Eva?)
in the bathroom
all we get are bathrooms
...actually, we don't even get those anymore either

all we get are Goodwill couches
*where else am I supposed to sleep*
demanded Lilith when she was evicted
only mildly comforted
when Eva showed up on her stoop
seven years later
seven years angrier

we get the brushing of dry elbows in line at the drop-in center
where they test for free
Lilith holds restless Eva's shaking earth-quaking hand
every goddam week
those demons are tricky, slippery, seductive
every day, a hundred more
*But they are my children,* Lilith will sigh in the tide
of the starless night
her mouth against the softest part of Eva's throat, chafing the skin
with her pumice lips
the whisper, too, is a demon

we get fire escapes
(an apt metaphor,
sneaking out the back door)
and the pounding of bare feet on metal
as Lilith's Goodwill couch becomes a torch
the volcanic wrath of stolen souls ignites what they have been told are rites
rites of passage, gilded tickets
Eva cools Lilith's broiling brow
every goddam night

*all we got is time*
watches spill from my mouth with every kiss
Lilith blames Eva for eatin' Eden
Eva cares less and less which witch she goes to bed with
they unravel each other's ends
unweave each other's threads
sewing machines in reverse
it is a competition, you see
who will be left
the last measly bit of cloth, proof that she won
with only a spool for company

## A Rage

The thunder sounds like
some foolish body tumbling down the metal stairs
the stairs
    the stairs
        the stairs
I've been told
God gets angry too

## Be safe

The first time I was told
to "be safe"
by another as strange as me
who looked me in the eye
with the unspoken words
*there are monsters out there who crave to devour you*
was when I left the queer oil wrestling basement party
for the silent and sexless cold of February
(but fuchsia gogo lights make everything a little more dramatic)
holding my Black lover's hand

Before then
my lovely Mid-Atlantic non-accent
the understood curve of my hips
the translucent ecru of my elbows
and wined lips
circled around me like a force field
as I walked through the raucous, broken glass-spangled night
made me
unthreatening
even as I crouched

It is not that
life is any more dangerous
with her by my side
I mean
it is not that
there are steel spikes or sinkholes
around the bed
that we must maneuver
I mean
there already was a minefield
in the bed
which we roll over
constantly
*ka-boom*

It is just that
there are some kinds of love
that come with a thick bark
dead, infected wood that needs
stripping away
It is just that
some people are afraid
of the breathing tree beneath
and would rather chop it down
than inhale its oxygen
It is just that
when I searched online for the names
of the lesbians murdered in Texas
(Crystal and Britney and Mollie and Kristene, three of whom were people of color)
I got porn instead
which tells me
exactly how we (but mostly she) are imagined and desired:
fucked dead

But it is equally seductive a lie
to think that I never learned this destruction
as one of its arms
carefully spinning webs of hatred of Blackness
the silver spools of taught thought taut in my fingers as I
seek to undo
the venom I acquired

*Be safe*
I wake up with one hand around my throat
and the other around hers
*There are monsters out there who crave to devour you*

# The Tale End

The novella-fairies heard
that there would be an inquisition
from George, the smallest one
who had been singing golden lattice patterns by the brook
when the Lieutenant Owl of the Legume Army passed her by
*(Long live the Bean)*

For a moment, all was still
as the novella-fairies surveyed their hive
tuning out poor whimpering George
But the proper course of action was quite obvious
The sweetest of nectar, the cruelest of waterfalls
They would not lie in wait
sitting fucks
*On vole comment?*
A briny irony that *steal* and *fly* are the same word
*We shall steal ourselves*
*soar into the sky, in pursuit of the moon*
*which we too shall steal*

There will be nothing left to take
when the legumes arrive.
There will be no answer
when the Lieutenant inquires.

## Dead Sea Blues

A diasporic Jew and a diasporic Palestinian walk into the Dead Sea.

(That is the punchline.)

"If things had worked out, I would be on the other side of this."
A pause.
"If things had worked out…"
Another.
"If things had worked out, I wouldn't exist."

Pain is volleyed for the other to catch, bear, and lay down so that
knees stay touching, rather than knuckles
Occupying together as the other has been occupied
There are ropes of blood that look strangely like graduation cords

Wading into the watery salt
makes my feet sting, the rocks blister under the unforgiving sun
(have I secretly loved the snow, admired her delicate power all along?)
but the burning brine, burning rubble
they say *Go from here*
*Go in peace, but go.*
That is fine, I will take my snow—I am a warm creation.

Across the way I see burning trees
(I had not realized water could be so flammable)
We splash each other
hoping to catch fire
but settling for the caustic saline scorch on our scalps
frying our hair like the hot irons of our youth
*In the name of assimilation*
*I command you to straighten*
Wanderer of wanderers
which odd did this queer beat
to meet
on the exile's side of the sea

A diasporic Jew and a diasporic Palestinian walk into the Dead Sea.

(They are the punchline.)

## DS 135 .P64 1893

Every Thursday at two
I go to the archive in the next city over
—the one with the bagels—
to read Leah Gritzman

This week the archive is being renovated
or demolished
there are walls missing
between the bookshelves
boxes overflowing with pages of testimony are strewn about
next week they will choose one to burn
to keep the furnace going

Pressed between two weary books

one on witches				the other on immigration
				she rests
waiting on home					waiting on me

In the finding aid
she is listed under "miscellaneous"
(women are confusing like that, the archivist tells me
I don't try to explain to him
that the catalogue was written by men)
but I memorized her call number long ago
as I memorized the rooster's footprints all over her face
the creases that taught me to tell the difference between laughter
and terror
for both will make the eyes crinkle
*So this is what my tsores bought?*
she asks me
(for I have my mother's everything)
I can only smile
though even that is pretty goyish

In lieu of running our bastard tongues
we sit side-by-side in the reading room illuminated by windows in the ceiling
though Leah will tell me we read by the light of my shiksa eyes
(I won't remind her that her grandson is the one
with the cobalt irises
which is what happens when your family crosses an ocean
children's eyes are like chameleons in that way)
and read until the dust settles
which is how we know the archive is closing for the day.

Until next week, Leah.

# About the Author

Farrell Greenwald Brenner is a queer troublemaker and Dana Scully enthusiast. She will graduate from Syracuse University in 2017 with a degree in women's & gender studies and citizenship & civic engagement. Her research focuses on the Aryan-passing women and girl couriers in the Jewish resistance movements of Nazi-occupied Poland, and she's also interested in the connections between Holocaust remembrance and Palestinian liberation. She has been the editor-in-chief of The OutCrowd Magazine, SU's LGBT publication, since the fall of 2014 and her work has also appeared in *The Feminist Wire* and *Lavender Review*. You can follow her kvetching on Twitter: @farrellelisms.

# Notes

"Cite This Poem: a performance in plagiarism" uses lines from the following poems, in this order:

Shel Silverstein, "Forgotten Language"
Walt Whitman, "O Captain! My Captain!"
Mahmoud Darwish, "In Jerusalem"
Audre Lorde, "A Litany for Survival"
Edgar Allen Poe, "Serenade"
William Shakespeare, "Sonnet 94"
Joy Harjo, "A Map to the Next World"
Robert Frost, "Stopping by Woods on a Snowy Evening"
Rumi, "On the Day I Die"
Margaret Atwood, "Helen of Troy Does Countertop Dancing."

# Acknowledgments

My thanks to the editors of the following publications, in which these poems first appeared:

*Lavender Review:* "Courted by the Snow"

*Perception Magazine:* "Red solo cup garden," "Dust," and "Library Smokers"

# Headmistress Press Books

*Lovely* - Lesléa Newman
*Teeth & Teeth* - Robin Reagler
*How Distant the City* - Freesia McKee
*Shopgirls* - Marissa Higgins
*Riddle* - Diane Fortney
*When She Woke She Was an Open Field* - Hilary Brown
*God With Us* - Amy Lauren
*A Crown of Violets* - Renée Vivien tr. Samantha Pious
*Fireworks in the Graveyard* - Joy Ladin
*Social Dance* - Carolyn Boll
*The Force of Gratitude* - Janice Gould
*Spine* - Sarah Caulfield
*Diatribe from the Library* - Farrell Greenwald Brenner
*Blind Girl Grunt* - Constance Merritt
*Acid and Tender* - Jen Rouse
*Beautiful Machinery* - Wendy DeGroat
*Odd Mercy* - Gail Thomas
*The Great Scissor Hunt* - Jessica K. Hylton
*A Bracelet of Honeybees* - Lynn Strongin
*Whirlwind @ Lesbos* - Risa Denenberg
*The Body's Alphabet* - Ann Tweedy
*First name Barbie last name Doll* - Maureen Bocka
*Heaven to Me* - Abe Louise Young
*Sticky* - Carter Steinmann
*Tiger Laughs When You Push* - Ruth Lehrer
*Night Ringing* - Laura Foley
*Paper Cranes* - Dinah Dietrich
*On Loving a Saudi Girl* - Carina Yun
*The Burn Poems* - Lynn Strongin
*I Carry My Mother* - Lesléa Newman
*Distant Music* - Joan Annsfire
*The Awful Suicidal Swans* - Flower Conroy
*Joy Street* - Laura Foley
*Chiaroscuro Kisses* - G.L. Morrison
*The Lillian Trilogy* - Mary Meriam
*Lady of the Moon* - Amy Lowell, Lillian Faderman, Mary Meriam
*Irresistible Sonnets* - ed. Mary Meriam
*Lavender Review* - ed. Mary Meriam

www.ingramcontent.com/pod-product-compliance
Lightning Source LLC
Chambersburg PA
CBHW070041070426

42449CB00012BA/3128